T0193761

Readjusting My Crown

Nicole Harris

authorHOUSE®

AuthorHouse™
1663 Liberty Drive
Bloomington, IN 47403
www.authorhouse.com
Phone: 1 (800) 839-8640

Published by AuthorHouse 06/20/2018

ISBN: 978-1-5462-4015-0 (sc)
ISBN: 978-1-5462-4039-6 (e)

Print information available on the last page.

This book is printed on acid-free paper.

Contents

Preface

Readjusting my crown is a compilation of how I used social media and journaling to find my purpose. In this thing called life, we are not giving clear cut directions on how to live life abundantly and successfully. To the world I may seem like I have everything together and under control. Heck, others have labeled me as strong. These adjectives are the furthest thing from being the truth. As part of my transparency, I wanted to share with the world how I found my purpose. This is only the beginning.

I received the highest degree in 2015, Doctorate of Education. I thought that life would be smooth sailing after obtaining this degree. Oh boy was I wrong. After receiving my doctoral degree all hell broke loose in my life. Or maybe now I had time to stop and pay attention to the things in my life. For two years, 2016 and 2017, my life was chaotic. I struggled with finding happiness at work and had to start going back to counseling because I no longer enjoyed what I did. When I walked away from my job, people closest to me thought I was absolutely insane for walking away. Who do you know that would walk away from a job as a leader with the freedom to come and go at will? Yes, me and I did. A job where the benefits outweighed the actual pay. To be honestly, I completely lost myself by throwing myself into a business that was not mine. I took care of someone else's baby and put my dreams on hold.

I struggled with passing the NCMHCE. The one thing that I wanted more than anything else was/is to become a LPC and do big things, but I was stuck at passing this exam. I continued to look at others that passed the exam and compare myself to them. I could not for the life of me understand how I could obtain a doctoral degree but could not pass this one exam and I came oh so close missing the mark by 3 points. The pain and hurt this caused me was unexplainable. One of my top goals was/is to become a LPC. I believe that I am a good therapist but I need this one thing to elevate me to the next level in my career. I even thought about going into an entirely different career.

Not only was I struggling with my career decisions but with my love life or should I say lack of a love life. I had been scarred by love and it just kept coming. The guy I fell in love with did not attend the most important day of my life, being hooded as Dr. Harris. This event was once in a lifetime and he did not show up. I felt as if I could not win for losing. This put a damper on things. And most importantly, he was having his own personal and professional issues that would hinder our relationship. I stepped back and allowed life to happen.

In 2016, I started posting "Doc's Corner" on Facebook and prior to that I would do an annual reflection on New Year's Eve. Doc's corner was developed as a way for me to cope with every day stressors. I use Doc's Corner to verbalize my frustrations as well as looking at the situation as a lesson learned. Doc's Corner is my platform to vent, to stand on my soapbox and to discuss how I feel with a little inspiration.

Nicole Harris

I did not realize that many of my "friends" on Facebook enjoyed reading my post. After positive feedback, I decided to make it a book to reach more people in hopes of inspiring them. This is part of my journey as Dr. Harris. On this journey, I had to readjust my crown more than once. I pray that this book helps you to look at life a little differently.

Love

Intro

I'm not very good at this thing called love. After my divorce from my high school sweetheart, I swore off love for a while. I've learned how to date myself and most importantly how to love myself. I will admit that a few have caught my attention but only a couple hold a place in my heart.

These passages provide a little insight on those men that were able to get close to me and hold a very special place in my heart. I wish I could tell you that these passages are about one man but of course with my luck these passages represent my interactions with three men in particular. All who hold a very special place in my heart. Even after failed relationship after failed relationship, I still believe in love.

With my knowledge and experience, I now know that a romantic relationship and even marriage is all about what the two individuals decide to make it. The individuals in the relationship will dictate how the relationship will be defined. We cannot compare our relationships to any other relationship, fictional or non-fictional.

These are my personal stories.....

LOVE

Relationships/Love
September 23, 2008

Hey:

I am sitting here reflecting on our friendship. I am at awe that you have recently admitted that you are growing extremely fond of me. It just amazes me. I pray that no matter what, that we will be able to maintain our friendship. You have been more than just a friend to me over the years; you have been my confidant, friend, lover, comforter just to name a few. You have truly played a major part in my life. Again, I am at awe that you have admitted how you feel about me. I guess, I always felt that this was a one-way street but over the last weeks you have proven me wrong. Thank you! It feels great to know that I am not alone on this emotional roller coaster.

Who would have guess that we would be so close? I still wonder what it is about you that keep me close. To name a few; there is something about your spirit, your personality, your attentiveness… I could go on but you get the picture. It amazes me that you were able to fill the void in my life without knowing exactly what I was missing. I know I never told you but then again it could have been the nonverbal clues. Just reflecting on how this all got started has me at awe. The scary part about our friendship/relationship has been the dreams I have had. I never told you about all of them in fact I don't think I told you about any of them. If only you knew. If the dreams come true I will tell you about them if not then the dreams were irrelevant.

Nicole Harris

Please know that I learned that you are a true friend who genuinely loves and care for me. I discovered that since I have been "ill" and I have heard the concern, worry, and fear in your voice as I share with you my symptoms and pains. You have been so supportive in all aspects of my life and I never had to ask, you just gave it to me. When I told you about going to therapy you were supportive. When I was in school you were supportive. When I needed a shoulder to cry on you were there. Again, you gave what I needed without me asking. You proved to me over and over again that chivalry is not dead. I hope this never ends but improve and flourish into a beautiful relationship.

At this point we both care dearly about each other; however, we are married to other people and we are unsure of the outcomes of these relationships. Deep in our hearts I know we both would like to end the drama but don't know how. If we were to ever be a serious couple I pray that we are able to keep the flames going and grow together. I also wonder when or if we become official and exclusive would our relationship remain the same, get stronger or deteriorate. Right now, I wonder if we are the way we are because of the suspense of our spouses or love ones finding out about us. Or is this the real thing? Or are we each other's scapegoats? Just questions to ponder. Well questions that I have pondered.

Love
December 2009

Have you ever looked into someone's eyes and saw all the pain and hurt they carry around and realize you can't help because they have to find their own peace and happiness? I have.

Love
March 2012

Have you ever met someone who… calmed you down just by their presence or voice, kiss on your forehead, was in tuned with your emotions, saw your emotional nakedness and still loved you for you…held you in their arms and melted away all you worries….touched you and made your heart race….held your hand and made the world disappear….when you cried they held you tighter….made you smile by just hearing their voice…..

Poem: Love
The Woman in Your Dreams
June 18, 2012

I'm the woman in your dreams but you are holding on to the past. I'm slipping out your grasp.

I'm the woman in your dreams the one who you see and your entire face light up, showing your pearly whites.

I'm the woman in your dreams that can hug away your pain and hurt.

I'm the woman in your dreams that you can't get enough of.

I'm the woman in your dreams but wait we've met before and you were holding on to your past. I'm slipping out your grasp.

While you were deciding which way to go, I was slowly slipping out your grasp.

Nicole Harris

If only you would have let go of your past, your dreams would be coming true because you were in my dreams too. But you continued to hold on to your past.

I am the woman in your dreams who you allowed to slip away.....

I was the woman of your dreams but you held on to your past too long and now I'm gone.

Poem: Love
I tried

July 29, 2012

I tried not to fall for you, I really did
At first I told myself that I couldn't be with a man like you
I tried not to fall for you
Unbeknown to me, you "walked" into my life as my then boyfriend was about to walk out
I tried not to fall for you
I put up my guard to ensure I would not fall for you
I tried really hard not to fall for you
Our conversations were sporadic
I tried not to fall for you
I watched you from the sideline admiring the man you are
I tried not to fall for you
I saw the emotional pain you carried
I tried not to fall for you
I saw a God fearing man; you made me want to talk in tongues
I tried not to fall for you

You started giving me hugs; you found my weakness…a warm embrace

I tried not to fall for you

I heard you say that you were not ready for a relationship

I tried really really hard not to fall for you

I tried to walk away, but something about you would not let me get too far

I tried not to fall for you

I thought it would be a long time before I was able to feel again but you came along

I tried not to fall for you

I tried to keep my feelings to myself but I can't anymore

I tried not to fall for you

I know you are not perfect you have flaws and emotional baggage but I admire you anyhow

I tried not to fall for you

I truly admire the man you are and the man that you will become

I tried not to fall for you

You are the first person I think of in the morning and the last person before I fall asleep

I tried not to fall for you

But every day I am falling for you, I'm falling

I know that this is not the direction you wanted our friendship to go

But I am falling for you

It was never my plan but I am falling for you

I tried to keep my feelings to myself but I just had to let you know, tomorrow isn't promised

I am falling for you

It was never my intention but I am falling for you

Nicole Harris

I thought about apologizing but why when love is the best gift to give…even when the person is not ready to give it in return

I am falling for you

LOVE
May 11, 2016

Doc's Corner:

You should be with someone that you CANNOT live without. Now that's deep. As women, we are raised to be very independent, so how can we find a man that we cannot live without? I can only speak for me as an independent woman. When the right man comes along you will know. He will cover you, protect you, pray for you, and pray with you. The right man will make you feel protected, respected, and loved. The right man will be your best friend and your biggest supporter. Not only will he support your dreams but he will also become the motivation and inspiration as well as encourager of your dreams. The right man will know what you do at work and encourage you when you are down. The right man will call to check on you. He will know your mood by the way you say "hello" when you answer the phone. The right man will take care of you when you are sick. The right man will respect you at all cost, will never call you out of your name even when he is upset with you. He will always treat you like his queen. The right man will not allow the sun to set with the two of you being upset with each other. The right man will kiss you on your forehead as a sign of adornment. When you find the right man, he will be your strength. #hewillfindme #lovemesomehim

Love
January 15, 2016

Doc's Corner:

If I ever get married again…. It will last forever. Sounds like a fairytale but I do still believe in the institution of marriage. I believe that marriage is an institution that allows a man and woman to share their lives by putting God first, supporting each other, loving each other unconditionally, sharing goals, working to achieve goals, and protecting each other from the world. So, if I ever get married again…. My future husband would have to have an intimate relationship with God in order to find me. He would have to love me with all my flaws, uniqueness, my accomplishments, and insecurities. My future husband would have to celebrate me. He would have to love my daughters as his own. He would have to treat me like a queen and be my king no my warrior. He will be focus, driven, and comfortable in his own skin. My future husband will think that I am the most gorgeous woman in the world, inside and outside. He will support me in my goals and dreams in fact he will make sure that he can help me to achieve my dreams and goals. Did I mention that my future husband would love God and will not be ashamed to confess his love for God or me? I will be his muse and he will be my strength!!! My future husband will not be intimidated by my emotional nakedness but embrace me and love on me. My future husband will not be ashamed to show public affectation, will profess his love for me in public, will be proud to call me his wife, will be my shoulder to lean on, and my best friend. He will not be intimidated

Nicole Harris

by my success and professional accomplishments. If I ever get married again, I will have a small intimate ceremony. I believe the walk down the aisle and the man seeing his bride in a beautiful dress is a symbolic ritual that should be done. If I ever get married again, I will make sure that I put all the cards on the table including the nonnegotiable items. If I ever get married again, we both would put God first and keep Him in our marriage. If I ever get married again, we will build an empire together and be like pinky and the brain!! LOL...I'm serious, we will build an empire and be the epitome of a power couple. We will give back to the community by sharing our individual stories as well as our story as a successful power couple. If I ever get married again, he will be in tuned with me and know how to make me smile, laugh, and enjoy life to the fullest. If I ever get married again, it will be forever. To my future husband, when God created me He broke the mold, I hope you are ready for me. You have to be ready to LOVE and LEAD as well as understand my personal struggles that helped to define the gorgeous woman that I am today. If I ever get married again......

Insecurities
April 15, 2016

Doc's Corner:

Insecurities plus lack of communication, understanding, and trust are relationship killers. Check your insecurities. Make sure you recognize your insecurities.

Relationships
April 17, 2016

Reflections of Friend-SHIPS

Facebook reminds individuals of memories, today my memory was of a dear friend that I truly adored. Sadly, he is no longer with us. This made me reflect on my limited friendships….my ship. I thank God for these individuals and I would not trade them in for the world. On this journey called life, I have had to face many obstacles, some I thought I would not make it through but each person in my circle played a role in keeping me grounded and aiding me through the obstacle. Again, I thank God for selecting these exceptional individuals for me. These individuals can honestly say that they know me…see those who know me, know my struggles, my pains, and my dreams as well as support me in my journey. While I see an ordinary person when I look in the mirror; they see an extraordinary woman. My ship wants me to share my story, excuse me my testimony with the world. My ship….sometimes see things that I don't see. The thing about my very small circle is that they cover me, protect me, pray for me, support me, and celebrate my accolades at all times. If you look at the dynamics of this circle of mine you will see how each person plays an integral part of my life….my journey….my destiny. These individuals are critical of those who come into my life and always err on the side of caution. To say that I trust and value these individuals' opinions is an understatement. These individuals keep me grounded. During the past week, I asked that while in public that a friend stop calling me

Nicole Harris

"Doc"….well I received a loving tongue lashing. I was told I worked too hard not to be called "Doc". I had to marinate on that for a minute…..I am Dr. Harris; however, to my friends I want to just me Nicole. Thankfully, my friends share a different view and will now and forever more call me "Doc"….. I love the respect of my circle….my ship. My friends and I are not crabs in a barrel, we are not defined by our titles but we define our titles. They also will let me know when they are leery or fond of a person who enters into my life. The great part about my ship….is that some of them operate on discernment and they are under the anointing…. You see a purpose of a ship is to aid in traveling long distance as well as protect, support, and cover you from the elements. My ship of friends do exactly that plus one more important element….we pray for each other. While Facebook reminded me of a friend that I lost….it also made me thankful of the friend-SHIPS that remain. To my close friends…..thank you for the covering me and the prayers…thank you for the support…thank you for seeing an extraordinary woman in me an ordinary woman. Thank you for keeping me grounded.

Relationships/Love
4/29/2016

Doc's Corner

Have an attitude of gratitude. I have had the opportunity to observe many situations and at the end of the day, we all need to have an attitude of gratitude. Be thankful for what you have and where you are in life. Yes, we all want more but in order to get bless with better and more we must be thankful and grateful for what we already have. I would love to have more and to have my cup overflowing with blessings but first I must show myself worthy. Most of us post on Facebook about the perfect no ideal relationship we would like to have. We like pictures that symbolize the "something" we want in our lives. Just remember much is given and much will be required. I am thankful that I am not who I use to be or where I use to be…..I have no problems working hard in order to get what has been promised to me.

Most of us post on Facebook about the perfect no ideal relationship we would like to have. Have you asked yourself if you were prepared to be an ideal partner? Are you ready for the work you have to put into this relationship? Lately, I have been seeing post in regards to the amount of time you have known someone versus how the two connect… "click". Don't let the representative fool you. You see the representative, play on everything that you said was lacking in your previous relationship. They use that to reel you in and once they have done so they let their guard down and you see the real them…. the representative has disappeared.

LOVE
May 9, 2016

Doc's Corner:

No one is every too busy for you. If they want to talk to you, text you, check on you….guess what they will make time for you!!! In this day and age there are numerous forms of communication….use one.

Dr. Harris is now off her soap box.

Nicole Harris

Love
June 2, 2016

Doc's Corner

Doc is back on her soapbox.

Let's talk about relationships and happiness. Yes, they go together like peanut butter and jelly.

First, you must be happy with yourself. You have to be happy with who you are with all your flaws and uniqueness. In my opinion, no person can complete you. They can complement you and keep you grounded. The two of you should be like yin and yang. In a relationship, you should be able to be yourself at all times. If your significant other does not understand you and try to change you; you may not be in the right relationship. Your significant other should support you, encourage you, pray for you and with you, challenge you intelligently to name a few.....Be leery of those who are extremely jealous, possessive, controlling...

Your relationship will not always be happy go lucky; however, it should be a safe haven.

Love
July 27, 2017

Doc's Corner

~Relationships~

In every relationship, there is give and take better yet deposits and withdrawals. I will admit that relationships are not 50/50, they are not easy, and no you shouldn't keep score. A healthy relationship is about positive deposits and withdrawals and yes challenges will come. A relationship is about finding balance…. where you are weak the other is stronger. Now, I am no expert on relationships but I know a thing or two about what makes a relationship fail. Since I know a thing or two about what helps destroy a relationship, I can infer that the opposite will flourish a relationship.

The follow are major components of any healthy relationship.

1. Open communication
2. Trust
3. Honest/openness
4. Respect
5. No judgement
6. Accountability (individually & Shared)
7. Listening for understanding
8. Healthy boundaries
9. Ability to express one's emotions
10. Agree to disagree
11. Enjoying quality with each other
12. Knowing the other's love language

The above components will help any relationship and I'm sure there are many more components that will help. If you come to the point that you are depositing a lot into the other person and they are withdrawing a lot from you and you have no more left for yourself or anyone else…….it's time to let, go. In any relationship, you have to love yourself before you can love anyone else. You have to be okay being alone before you will be okay being with someone else. Remember 'ships can and do sink…. No matter the kind of 'ship.

Nicole Harris

LOVE
October 2, 2017

Lately you have been on my mind Cassius. It has been 2 years 3 months since you died. Oh boy, I miss you like crazy…. The last couple of months you have been in my spirit…. You were the only man that knew something was wrong by the way I said "hello" when I answered the phone or by what I texted you. We were not perfect in fact we had our issues but we loved each other unconditionally. I miss you like crazy…. I know I keep saying that but I do. I miss our phone conversations….our public interactions…. The fondest memory was when we were in the grocery store and you said you would love me if I only had a high school diploma. Here I am with a doctoral degree and I don't have that special someone in my life…. No not you but that special love that I need. You always told me that I was… I am wife material and men know that. So, I guess that's why I'm single …. I must truly intimidate these men. Cassius Sutton, how I miss you. I missed your hugs… they melted away all my cares, worries, and concerns. I regret our last good bye….. you came over it had to be around Easter time or something like that because you came to the house and said you knew I cooked. I fixed you a plate and you ate…. My friend at the time called while you were here and I talked to him instead of you…. I'm so sorry. I wish that things would have been different between us. Cassius Sutton, I love you today and forever….continue to rest in peace my love.

A Change is Gonna Come
October 6, 2017

Many great entertainers have belt the lyrics to this classic song, "A Change is Gonna Come." I dare not try to say who did it better, they were all great in their own right. Nevertheless, this title has been in my spirit for quite some time. I haven't been able to shake it…. I hope I can do it justice.

A change is gonna come…. It's already setup for the change to occur whether it's financial, spiritual, professional, intimate relationship, personal relationships, or mentally …. A change is on its way.

There is power in the tongue…. Speak positivity into existence. I stopped by to tell you that a change is gonna come…. It's been too long….What I have discovered in this world to be true for me is that I have to have an intimate relationship with the High Most…my God. I've been slacking a little. Once I get back where I know I belong everything else will fall into place. My change is on its way.

But I came to talk to you about intimate relationships. This has been a hot topic in my inner circle. Based on my circle of friends, I have learned that when a woman loves a man she will stand beside him until he pushes her away. The ladies in my circle want to build an empire with the man she is in love with. Yes, we want you to bring something to the table; however, what you don't have we can obtain it together. We want to have your undivided attention… we want you to ask us how was our day, how are you feeling, to hug us, to love on us, to spend quality time with us, to support us…. My circle of friends are not worried about

Nicole Harris

material things; we are interested in building and investing with the one we love. Fellas, if your lady has been by your side and continues to ask for the same thing over and over and over again and you fail to comply… If her arguments turn into silence, if her cries turn into staying at work later than the norm, if she no longer calls you to check on you…. please know she has given up. Once she has given up and decided to walk away there is nothing you can do. One thing about women by the time you noticed that they are tired of all your lies and neglect, she has already made plans to exist without disrupting her life.

WORTHY
Doc's Corner
October 8, 2017

Lately, my dear friend has been on my mind (may he rest in peace). We had numerous conversations about relationships but the one that stands out … is when he kissed me on my forehead and told me a man knows when he meets a woman if they are (1) a toy … just someone to play with (2) a keeper…. Wife material. He finished the conversation with "Baby girl you are a keeper." I needed and wanted to know the particulars on this subject. The only other information he would share with me is that when a man meets a woman he knows which category she is in.

Fast forward to the present…. My inner circle & I have been talking about interpersonal relationships for a while now. Ladies, the men that we love know our WORTH! They just don't think we have the courage to leave because they know we love them to life. These men have forgotten that what they did to get us they need to do that and more to keep us. Yes, ladies they took us for granted. These men know how we love but don't pay attention to the warning signs. We no longer argue with them, we no longer rush home to take care of them, our answers turn into sheer silence, and we become numb to the hurt these men, we love, have caused us. Yes ma'am, your man knows your WORTH....he just never thought you would leave or even think about leaving him. From the moment he saw you and held that initial conversation with you....he knew you were a keeper. Unfortunately, he hasn't learned how to keep you. You are everything he wants but he can't handle the qualities that made him fall in love with you. He knows your WORTH! Sorry ladies but sometimes they learn a day too late. Sometimes men have to lose everything to realize what they had.

Summary

You just had a glimpse of my love and relationships. You may have noticed that I am a hopeless romantic with a hint of reality. I had to read and reread these passages and I must admit that I relieved each moment and knew which man I was referring to. This thing called love is just amazing. I no longer believe my knight in shining armor will come and recue me. However, my king is on his way. My king will not be as I "ordered" but everything I need and more. Until my king arrives, I will continue my journey walking on faith.

Nicole Harris

Faith

Faith…. For as long as I can recall I have always believed in a higher power, Jesus Christ. Yes, my faith has wavered but at the end of the day I know whose I am. This journey called life has taken me on a rollercoaster ride. This rollercoaster ride as landed me prostrate, on my knees, and any other position praying that things would get better. There were times when I have fought everything God wanted me to do just to surrender all to Him. I am still seeking to find my purpose in this world. My plan for my life has fallen completely apart… I have to trust in God. His plan is so much greater than mine.

Jeremiah 29:11 (NIV)

Faith
September 24, 2012

My inner circle, me included have been going through for about a year or so…my response has always been stand still & wait on the Lord after yesterday's sermon I can add …. and see through your spiritual eyes (Exodus 14:13-14). The decisions you make are between you & God…and you have to live with that decision. Don't let everyone's opinion deter you from making the best decision for your life.

Happiness
October 19, 2015

Doc's Corner:

Happiness
Happiness is a mental and emotional state. It is also a choice that each of us make every day, consciously or subconsciously. Yes, environmental and emotional stimuli may affect how you feel. It's still a choice. Yes, you will have bad days. I encourage you to look at the glass as half full; choose happiness. I will be the first to admit that I have had some bad days, people have talked about me well they still do, people have lied on me, and I have had days where I wanted to do nothing more than cry. Every day I wake up, I decide to be happy regardless of what is going on internally or externally. Yes, I know you aren't at the financial status you would like. I know you don't have the career, house, or even car that you want. But choose happiness. Don't get me wrong, some days it is hard to be happy especially when everything seems to be going wrong all around you but please choose happiness over the alternative of sadness, anger, worry, and any other negative emotion. Let's weigh the consequences…...happiness does not cause any physical ailments. However, sadness, anger, and worry can actually cause physical ailments. Trust me, I know when I have any other emotion besides happiness my fibromyalgia flares up and my body tells me that I need to change my mood ASAP. So again, I say HAPPINESS is a CHOICE!!!! I encourage

Nicole Harris

you to CHOOSE HAPPINESS…..no matter your situation or circumstance be HAPPY. You are in control of your EMOTIONS…..no one else has the power or ability to make you HAPPY but YOU.

Free Will
February 21, 2016

Doc's Corner

Free Will
The phrase "free will" has been in my spirit for a while and I am not 100% sure why. To help me to understand "free will" let's process it. Proverbs 16:9 states that a "man's heart formulates his way but the Lord directs his steps". Let's see if I can break this verse down. So, God allows us to make our own decisions. God allows us to use our own free will to decide if we want to stay or go; if we want to forgive or not; if we want to be happy or not; etc. Even though it is our free will to make whatever decisions we choose our Heaven Father will order our steps. Powerful…....So no matter our decision God will make it work for our good. Now how awesome is that…. how wonderful is our Father that He will ensure that something works out for our good? You see right here you should be praising God and thank Him for just being God!!!!

Let me try to correlate this verse to a relationship, since we all have relationships. As for me, I am trying to make sure that the next relationship I am in moves to the next level and last forever.

So, a man and a woman are in a relationship for about 2 years. One person wants to take the relationship to the next level and the other does not. Both individuals have free will to choose as they please. The person that wants to take the relationship to the next level has the option to wait for the other person to get "ready" or move on. The same goes for the person that is not ready to take the relationship to the next level, they can decide to walk away or stay. Each person has free will and no matter the choice they make, God will order and guide their steps. Hmmm... I could be in a relationship and love my man and he does not want to take it to the next level. And if I choice to walk away God will order my steps. Now that is a wonderful Father. I feel as if this is where Romans 8:28 comes in…... Romans 8:28 states that "all things work together for good to them that love God, to them who are called according to his purpose". …… If I make a decision according to my heart, God will order my steps….and He will make sure that all things work out for the good.

Well now…. I'm getting off my soap box. Please note that I was trying to make sure that I understand "free will" according to this verse…....if I am wrong please advise me. I don't know who needed this.

Grateful
April 2, 2016

Doc's corner:

I am thankful for this journey called life. I may not be where I want to be but thank God I am not where society says I should be. According to society, I should not have a doctorate degree. You see society counted me out at the age of 18 when I had my first child. But I am a daughter of the

King. My Father sits high and looks low. When the world counted me out, I went to my Heavenly Father….. and because I can do all things through Christ who strengths me (Philippians 4:13), I am where I am today. Please know that I had some trials and tribulations during this journey. Once I became a mother….. I knew I had to push myself because I always had eyes on me. During my undergrad years, my daughter Alexis would go to class with me. When I graduated with honors, she was there to witness my success. In 2006, when I decided to go back to school…. I had to do all of this for two daughters now. When I graduated with my master's degree both of my daughters were able to see my success. I wanted my daughters to have a tangible hero….so I worked hard to become their superhero. I continued my education, I had some hiccups along the way….I became sick. However, I allowed my daughters to see my pain, my tears, my downs, and my ups. My daughters saw me staying up all night to complete a terminal degree. I did all of this and will continue to do even more so that my daughters, nieces, nephews, and godchildren will see how an individual becomes successful in a world that has counted them out. I pray that I am their superhero. Through this journey, I have held numerous titles but the one that means the most is "mother". To my daughters, Alexis and Jacqueline…. I pray that I am your superhero. I am still striving to reach my goals as well as living a life pleasing to our Heavenly Father. Please know that if I overcome diversity so can you. Go into the world and do great things. There is no limit to where you can go…I believe in you and your dreams. Love always mom

Faith

December 31, 2016

Doc's Corner

2017---> 2+0+1+7=10; 10 is completion; perfect so is the number 7; whatever you have been working on will be completed in 2017!

I pray that we all have a wonderful 2017, may our Father continue to bless us and we continue to bless each other. Share your gift and your knowledge.

Faith

January 7, 2017

Doc's Corner:

On this snowy day, I took the opportunity to review my FB profile. One post stood out: "The anointing that's on your life attracts attacks! Don't look at it as trouble, look at it as confirmation! Keep moving!"

Well, it has been confirmed! When God wants you to move and you refuse to move; He will make your situation get a little harder and the longer you stay the harder it will get. The more you try to be what that person, agency, etc. wants you to be the more uncomfortable you will become…. God is counting on that uncomfortableness… He knows that the only way you will move is to make you uncomfortable in your situation. Move, jump, and allow God to actually take the wheel…. take your hands off of it!!!

You were uniquely created…...be uniquely you.

Thank you to Clarice Edwards, Tarsha Debrough- Mae,

Nicole Harris

Mykia Grant, Timeeka Colvin, Monica Caldwell for encouraging me to be uniquely me. Much love to you ladies.

Faith
January 13, 2017

Doc's Corner:

I'm not sure who this is for but this scripture has been in my spirit all day.
Psalms 105:15 "Do not touch my anointed ones; do my prophets no harm."

Faith
February 27, 2017

Doc's Corner:

I believe we all have songs, scriptures, & topics that could describe our current status.
Topic: Your ordinary is someone else extraordinary.
Song: Too close to the mirror by Eddie Ruth Bradford
Scripture: Jeremiah 29:11

Faith
March 6, 2017

Doc's Corner:

When God takes you out of your comfort zone....you will never be the same. God will block any effort of going back! God is pushing you to your destiny. The more you fight God the harder it will become. Be who God created you to be.... uniquely you

Faith
March 12, 2017

Doc's Corner

Crossroads......

hmmm..... I had to sit in the middle of my crossroad because I did not know which way to go. I called on the only name that I knew would hear me... "Jesus". I played in my mind everything that anyone has ever said to me.... "you will never be anything," "you are always angry," "why are you so mean?" Oddly enough only the negative things seem to stand out. So, as I sat in the middle of my crossroad, I had a little talk with Jesus and told him all about my problems. I heard Him say you have served your purpose at this place, it's time to move on... of course me being the child I am ask but what will I do. Jesus replied I will supply all your needs and when the time is right I will open the door... don't be afraid because I am with you. Then positive thoughts ran through my head from previous supervisors....and I had to realize that sometimes what we go through isn't all for us but for the people watching us... I am walking in my purpose; my ordinary is someone else's EXTRAordinary. I may not be where I wanted to be but I am where I am suppose to be ....walking in MY purpose.

Nicole Harris

Faith
March 18, 2017

Doc's Corner:

So, I'm back on my soapbox. Today's theme was "Who are you following?"

I'm glad you asked. I am following the High Most, the Great I am, the King of Kings, the Bright Morning Star, my Solid Rock.... Jesus Christ!! In my short journey called life I have realized one important thing. What God has for you is for you!!! No one can do what God created for you to do.

I may not be what you think I should be but I am everything that God created me to be. I will not conform to your opinion of me. I will be unapologetically me... Dr. Nicole Harris with all my flaws.

Faith
May 21, 2017

Doc's Corner

We are half way into 2017. . . for some it has been a cruise and for others it has been a bumpy roller coaster ride. For those that are going through a storm.... I urge you to stay the course. Yes, things can get a little rocky, you will have some weary days, some nights you may cry yourself to sleep, and maybe some lonely nights. Please, stay the course. About 20 years ago, during one of my storms.... a lady told me something that I have never forgotten: "God will never give you anything that you can't handle." This lady didn't know my situation but her words left an imprint on my life. While at times I may question that very statement and wonder what strength do I have that I'm not aware of…. but through it all I stayed the course. When things get rough in your life be prepare with a game plan. Where do you find that peace? In music, a place, a smell, a scripture, spirituality, religion, or a combination. Where you find your peace, go to it during your storm and hold on… Trouble don't last.

Psalm 23:5 (KJV) ~ Thou preparest a table before me in the presence of mine enemies: thou anointest my head with oil; my cup runneth over.

Other scriptures that encourage me are: Jeremiah 29:11; Psalm 42; Proverbs 3:4-5

I'm so glad that my Father sits high and looks low… that He forgives me more times than I care to count… that He is Alpha and Omega…...

Faith
June 21, 2017

Doc's Corner

When God says move you move
No! Let me put in a different way "When He moves you move just like that."

2017 has taught me to move when God say move. When you don't move when God tell you to move life gets a little hard and you find yourself making unorthodox decisions. This year I have stood, sat, laid at the crossroad a many of nights. My problem was trying to please man… let me repeat that… my problem was trying to please man. One day the light bulb came on and I realized that I could only do what God created me to do. During my moment of weakness, I agreed to do something that was not my talent and I failed. Heck, I wasn't bothered because I knew that wasn't for me. In October 2016, God told me to move and I flat out refused. I told God I wasn't ready, I had more work to do where I was. I believe God just chuckled at me. I'm that hard-headed child, so I had to learn the hard way. From Oct 2016 to Jan 2017, things got real rough…... I mean real rough. I finally told God I give up, I'll listen. God asked me to move just like that…. After hours of crying, days of questioning God…. I finally moved just like that. I'll admit God never ever told me it would be easy… He wanted to know if I would follow Him and His instructions. Please know that there is always a test. Interview after interview, job offer after job offer, test after test, God is always up to something. But when He shows up...He shows out!!! I took a job that I did NOT want for the sake of having a job. God asked me why did I accept that position. Me being me said I needed to take care of my family. Do you know what God said? Yep…. He said He will supply all of my needs. Welp… there you have it. I suppose to move when God tells me to move. Needless to say, God placed me where He wanted me. And yes…He continues to test me every day. So, when God say move please move. Galatians 1:10 (NIV) says: "Am I now trying to win the approval of human beings, or of God? Or am I trying to please people? If I were still trying to please people, I would not be a servant of Christ."

Stop trying to please people and following the "in" crowd; God created you to stand out. Be uniquely you…. You will enjoy this life a whole lot better when you do. Besides life is too short to try to be like everyone else.

~Doc Harris~

Faith

July 13, 2017

DOC's Corner

You're right where you belong; the storm is just a lesson

After having a conversation with God, He gave me this topic. So, me being the child I am started asking questions. God's response was powerful (but of course). He sent me to Proverbs 3:5 "Trust in the Lord with all your heart and lean not on your own understanding". Ok God, I get that but this is hard. I don't know how much more I can bear. So, my Heavenly Father asked me when was the last time I read Psalm 55:22? I looked around and picked up the bible and turned to Psalm 55:22 "Cast your cares on the Lord and he will sustain you; he will never let the righteous be shaken". I don't know about you but I have real conversations with God. God and I had this conversation and I was pretty much like God you have too much faith in my ability to sustain this storm, this lesson… I can't handle this. I can't do this. God chuckled at me and said my dear daughter have you forgotten what is in your instructional guide (B.K.A the bible). Of course, I am speechless. God being God then asked me what does my signature line say on my email…. Matthew 19:26 "With God all things are possible" Our conversation goes on…. But I want to focus on You're right where you belong.

For those who are near and dear to me know that I have been struggling to pass the LPC exam. The last two weeks or more God have given me clarity. It boils down to this: I am right where God wants me to be. I am a mentor,

Nicole Harris

educator, role model, motivator to those around me. See I had to see this and understand this before God will elevate me to the next level. I had to come to the terms that God created me uniquely to be me. I'm always saying that I am an unorthodox counselor but I never thought about it as it related to my personal life. I had to come out of my comfort zone to be able to see how my presence can possibly change the situation. I was told since I've started this new job that I have changed the atmosphere. My supervisees have told me that they have learned more from me in the last 3 months than any other supervisor. I have been asked how can you motivate others when you are going through your own storm. Well about 11 years ago, a great friend told me that what I was going through wasn't for me but for others to see how I handle my situation. Ever since that comment I have tried my best to motivate and encourage others when I can even when I don't feel like it, even when no one motivates me. I am RIGHT where God wants me to be!!! I may not be where I want to be or think I should be but I am at the right place. I cannot worry about what this person over there is doing because that's their journey and not mine... I can only be who God created and ordain me to be and that's Dr. Nicole Harris with all my flaws.

You are RIGHT where God wants you to be, embrace it, learn your lesson, thank God, be grateful you are no longer the person you use to be......

Faith
August 22, 2017

Doc's Corner

You can't... but I can

A few weeks ago, a friend and I were having a conversation about resigning.... quitting a job. She stated that men and women should not quit a job unless they have another one to replace it. I chuckled. While in this world that is a great practice; however, sometimes God put you in a place where you are uncomfortable so that you will trust only Him. In January, I stepped out on faith... I left a job where I had reached the glass ceiling. It was one of the hardest decisions I have ever made... but today as I reflect a little more on that decision it was for self-preservation, it was because my time was up, I had completed my task and it was time to move forward.... My tenure at that agency taught me so much but the most important thing was to never put my all into an agency that does not belong to me... I will always put my best foot forward. The thing about my resignation was I knew three months prior that it was my time to go but me being the child I am did not want to hear it. I was comfortable where I was...so God started to make it uncomfortable so I would step out on faith. As I write this I am reminded of Jeremiah 29:11 - 14 "God has plans to prosper us". Staying when God told me to move could have blocked my blessings.

But God.... While the world says, you can't God says you can. You just have to lean on God for understanding (Proverbs 3:5-6). I truly believe that you have to do what is

Nicole Harris

best for you at that very moment… that you have to know whose you are and that God did not create us to be fearful (2 Timothy 1:7). I wish I would have listened to God when He was whispering it's time to go but instead I waited until He was yelling, and I had to move quickly. I did not know how I was going to make it but I heard God say that I will supply all your needs (Philippians 4:19).

Don't allow anyone to tell you …. You can't. When they say, you can't reply but I can and I will.

"Have I not commanded you? Be strong and courageous. Do not be afraid; do not be discouraged, for the Lord your God will be with you wherever you go." Joshua 1:9

Forgiveness
9/2/2017

Doc's Corner

I forgive you….no me

I forgive you…no me for not listening when you said you were not ready instead I waited around for four years…... I forgive me

I forgive you . . . no me for allowing you to belittle me when I know my worth. I forgive me.

I forgive you….no me for listening to your lies knowing damn well you were lying to me. I forgive me.

I forgive you….no me for thinking we were friends when all you wanted was to take my position. It's yours. I forgive me.

I forgive you….no me for not effectively communicating my needs. I forgive me.

I forgive you....no me for not speaking up when you put me on the back burner. I forgive me.

I forgive you….no me for allowing you to make me an option. I forgive me.

I forgive you….no me for allowing your negativity to get into my spirit…for believing that I would never amount to anything. I forgive me.

I forgive you….no me for allowing you to put a damper on one of the most important days of my life…. I thought you knew the importance of the day…. silly me…. I finally forgave myself.

I forgive me for forgetting my worth, for not standing up for what I want, for not effectively communicating my wants and needs, for not listening…. I finally forgive me. My strength to forgive myself has empowered me to say good bye to the ship we had and face what is yet to come.

I wanted closure from all these relationships but I have never gotten them from these individuals. At this point in my life I have to forgive me for allowing these behaviors…. for not speaking up. I can no longer wait on someone else to provide me closure. For now, on I will gain my own closure…. I will forgive me for allowing this foolishness to go on in my life.

Who do you need to forgive? Do you need closure from a past relationship? How do you plan on healing your wounds? Have you written them a letter? Have you sought therapy? What have you done?

~Bear with each other and forgive one another if any of you has a grievance against someone. Forgive as the Lord forgave you. ~ Colossians 3:13

Faith
Where is your faith?
January 29, 2018

Last night, during a regular conversation with a close friend I was asked: where is your faith? He stated: The lady I met a few years ago always put God first. I saw that lady go through so much and did not worry because of her faith. He went on to tell me that it seems as if I lost my faith a little more than a year ago. He took me on this journey from the time we met to present and asked what happened to my faith. I'm so thankful that we were on the phone because the tears were now flowing quickly from my eyes. This time I answered his question. Oh, my faith it's still here. I assure you, it's at least the seed of a mustard seed. Recently, my disappointments, embarrassments, and wrong choices have out shine my faith. Now why did I say that …. he went to his favorite description of me (just my perspective.) He said you are one of the strongest women I know. I tried my best to tell him I am not strong. (I am not a fan of this adjective as it relates to me) So, he went on to ask me a series of questions. I attempted to go around the questions but at the end of the day from his *perspective* I am strong.

This gentleman and I have been friends for at least five years and this was an emotional roller coaster of a conversation. He knows me well enough to "check" me and address …. confront the things that I am dealing with. After we hung up all I could say is "but God". Only God could have orchestra a conversation like this.

I am intentional on being reserved about my faith and expressing my love for the Father, Son, and Holy Spirit as I once did. Why? Because I have fallen so far from grace and I am so embarrassed of the choices that I have made and I did not involve the Father in any decision that I feel bad about inviting him into my mess. Yes, I know in Matthew 18:22 the Lord God say forgive seventy times seven…. But I am my worse critic. And before you quote Psalms 55:22 to me…let me say this, my spirit being knows and understands that if I take my burdens to God and leave them there He will supply all my needs…my issue is with this flesh that walks on the earth and have to interact with the people of the world. Even a child of the High Most gets weary … I am the first to admit that I lost focus … and so now I am in the place of realigning my sight upon the Lord… I had started looking down too long and fear consumed me. Fear that I was not good enough, fear that I was not walking into my purpose, fear that I would be everything that the naysayers said I would be, fear that I would not be able to get my footing, fear that God would not forgive my sins because I continued to sin daily. Oh, my list could go on and on. Some days I sit and wonder if I am like the psalmist Eddie Ruth Bradford song "Too Close to the Mirror" …. Am I too close to mirror to see what God sees in me? As I end this I am reminded of Isaiah 40: 31 "But they that wait upon the LORD shall renew their strength; they shall mount up with wings as eagles; they shall run, and not be weary; and they shall walk, and not faint".

Summary

What can I say about my faith that you haven't read? Well, I will be the first to tell you that these eloquent words surely did not come from me. I reviewed these words and was in awe. They are powerful and still relevant. My faith has wavered but I continue to have a faith the size of a mustard seed. I've stepped out on faith and still depending on God. The years 2016 and 2017 has be hard from me beyond words, to the point that I had to do some self-reflecting. But l am thankful that know whose l am.. l am a daughter of the King of kings.

Self-Reflection

A few years back, I decided to reflect on my life and how far I have come. What better time to complete this self-reflection then on my birthday and New Year's Eve. This journey called life has been a real challenge for me. So, I ease the pain by reflecting on my journey and how far I have come on this journey. NO, I'm not where I want to be but thank God, I'm not who I use to be. As cliché as it may be my self-reflections has shown me that I've come too far to turn around now. Every year my self-reflections become more transparent and the more transparent they become the harder it is for me to show my vulnerability to the people around me. Doc's Corner has become a healthy outlet for me to show that this strong, educated, independent woman could also be vulnerable in a public platform….such as Facebook.

Self-Reflection
February 29, 2012

Reflection….. This journey has not been easy. I've made friends and lost friends; some have made everlasting footprints in my heart, some were only here for a season and no matter their purpose in my life I will always appreciated the time we had together. I have made decisions that I never thought I would have made. I have accomplished tasked that I thought I could not. I have endured the storm and rain. I've had many struggles. I am infamous for putting on a façade as if I was a super hero. I fall but by the grace and mercy of God I get up. I have become a phenomenal woman. I have no regrets and I would not change a thing in my life.

Self-Reflection
August 1, 2013

As I get closer to turning another year older, I am taking a moment to reflect on the past 364 days. First and foremost, I am thankful for God's grace and mercy. I decided to be me at all times and I have done just that! I have gain some wonderful friends and lost some so-called friends. I have been through the storm but I still stand. Despite my situation, I am at peace. I will praise God in the hallway until the next door is opened for me. I have truly been blessed. Tomorrow, my birthday, will be wonderful!

Self-Reflection
December 30, 2013

Reflection of 2013….
1. My happiness is imperative to ME!!!!!
2. God answers prayers….right on time
3. Blessings will not come prematurely
4. God calls radical people to spread His word
5. What is for me is for me…no one else will get what God has ordained for me.

6. When someone loves you....they will love you with your flaws and all

7. I'm certified by God

8. She who kneels before God can stand before anyone

9. 2014 will be great....

10. Blessed by the best...I know whose I am

HAPPY NEW YEAR!!!!!

Self-Reflection
March 9, 2015

Daily reflection: I had to stop and look at my life.....I realized that I am blessed by the best. The enemy came to steal, kill, and destroy but God's grace and mercy covered me. #blessedbeyondbelief So thankful...not many know my story. #ihaveatestimony

Self-Reflection
December 29, 2015

This picture edifies 2015 for me..... no not the regalia but the raw emotion that is displayed in this photo.

Nicole Harris

Thanks Joyner Dream Catchers for capturing this raw emotion for me. Do you see it? The burden being lifted off her shoulders….The peace that the Lord of Lords has given her….Jehovah-Shalom

My dissertation contains two scriptures; one at the commencement of the acknowledgements and one at the end. They are as follows: "For I know the plans I have for you," declares the Lord, "plans to prosper you and not to harm you, plans to give you hope and a future." Jeremiah 29:11 (NIV) "As iron sharpens iron, so one person sharpens another." Proverbs 27:17 (NIV)

Reflection of 2015

I have learned….

As a mother, you can only instill values and morals in your child. Once they become of age, pray that God will cover them daily. I've done the best I could…the rest is up to them.

As a sister, God gave me one of the dearest friends who understand my upbringing because we share the same parents. Thank God for sisters. I love my big sister to life. She is one of my biggest fans. I never thought we would have an amazing relationship.

As a daughter, no matter how old you are your mother will ALWAYS have your back and be there to encourage you, love you, and support you. My mother is elated that I have accomplished all of this … watching her at my graduation, one would have thought she earned my degree.

As a friend, when you hit rock bottom and want to give up your true friends will be there to encourage you and pull you up. In this lifetime, you do not get many true blue friends. I am truly blessed to be surrounded by women that want to uplift me instead of standing on me. Thank you ladies. I am blessed to have a few... I do mean a few good male friends that also supported me and made sure that no harm came to me. Thank you.

As a leader, everyone cannot handle a blunt and direct leader. And no matter what you do a subordinate will blame you for their shortcomings. Very few people truly understand the phrase "business is business." It takes a special person to be able to be friendly and the boss at the same time and very unique people to be able to handle it.

I've learned that people in my culture are extremely proud of success and accomplishments. Since August, I have been called Dr. Harris every day...more by my elders than any other age group. I ran into one of my professors from NSU and I told him of my recent achievement and he stood up and said congratulations. I am still at awe. I am still trying to grasp this. My employer calls me Doc....I have to get use to this one.

I've learned that life is too short to be unhappy. My dear friend, Cassius departed from this world too soon. Because of his journey and struggles, I refused to be unhappy or allow the world to steal my joy. If I love you, I will tell you as often as I can. No one is promised tomorrow. Guys, please don't let your pride get between you and the woman you love. Life is too short. Happiness is a state of mind and determination.

I've learned that the heart wants what the heart wants but the mind has to be strong enough not to settle for anything less than the best.

Nicole Harris

I've learned ….. no it was confirmed that what God has for me is for me. No one can do what God has created for you better than you. God's plan is greater than any plan you can image for yourself.

Jehovah-Jireh

Self-Reflection
August 4, 2016

I'm another year older. I usually do my self-reflection in private; however, this year I decided to share it publicly.

I am absolutely in love with the woman I am today. You see it took me years to love Nicole Harris. Internally, I was fighting against what the world thought I should be and what others thought I should be until one day I decided to embrace my uniqueness. I love the lady God created me to be. She is more than I could ever image. I am not the crying baby my family remember me as, I am not the moody teenager my peers meet years ago, I am not the giggly young adult my ex-husband married, or the woman that got fire from a job. I am a hurt, abused, heartbroken woman that have stood up against adversity all because of Jesus Christ. My Eternal Rock has provided me with mercy and grace that I may stand today as Dr. Nicole Harris. My journey to this place hasn't been easy in fact most would say I shouldn't be here. I shouldn't be Dr. Nicole Harris but God. I am at awe at my own journey. Teenage mother, young wife, sickly, unemployed, rocky marriage, grad student, suicidal, divorcee, brain tumor, heartbroken, college grad times 4, lied on, talked about, abused, and just plain old life. Yes, I admire and love Dr. Nicole Harris and the woman she is. I may not be what you thought I should be but thank God I'm everything He wanted me to be. I have 2 beautiful daughters that I love to life. I am not afraid to be alone because that's when I learned how to truly love me for me. I have a small yet supportive circle that helps push me forward. I have a man in my life that loves me for me and is very supportive. I love my life and I love the woman that I am today. Tomorrow, I will be a slightly different woman and I will love her even more.

~Reflections~

Self-Reflection
December 31, 2016

Reflection of 2016

I honestly thought, I wouldn't be able to do my reflection for 2016 for so many reasons…. but God. I am assuming that my reflections help, touch, or moving people. Thank God!

This year I lost my focus….

I lost my focus, I'm not sure how or when it happened but it did and it slowed my journey down. This year I felt as if I was in a large storm… you know sometimes there was wind and obstacles and sometimes it was calm and quiet. The storm invaded all facets of my life and it took me for a wild ride that I don't ever want to get on again.

I lost focus …. On my Heavenly Father. I almost forgot that He sits high and looks low. That He is Alpha and Omega, Bright and Morning Star, I am, Redeemer, Jesus of Nazareth, Rock, Jehovah-Jireh, Jehovah-Shalom…. I lost my focus on my Heavenly Father…I fell for the worldly views and what the world wanted me to believe instead of the WORD.

I lost focus…. On me!! For a moment or three I forgot whose I am. I lost focus that I am the child of the Most High. That I am a daughter of the King of Kings. That I was created in His image. I am anointed by God. I got caught up in the worldly world… I started listening to the naysayers, to the haters, to the nonbelievers…. I felt like David in Psalms 42.

I lost focus…... of my purpose. I put my energy and time in someone's else dream…their baby… I am raising their child for them and they are enjoying the fruit…. but it's still part of the Master's plan. I put more energy into their baby that I forgot that I had to conceive and birth my own… to the point that I failed a much needed exam not once, not twice but three times. As I reflect on this journey….it was one for the Father, the Son, and the Holy Ghost. It is now time to focus on my dream, my destiny, God has been preparing me to give "birth" to my "baby" …the "baby" that will exemplify the Power of God.

I lost focus…. I had to take several seats to reflect not just on the last 365 days but my lifespan. Join me on this journey….a teenage mom….did I mention that that baby is now in college [insert praise here], graduated from college not once but four times….from teen mom to doctoral degree [insert praise here], diagnosed with fibromyalgia (2008), pituitary tumor and the list of health problems goes on and on but God [insert praise here], diagnosed with depression and anxiety….want to quit my job… but once I look back on my life and all that God has done for me and how far I have come. I had to thank God. And got some new glasses to regain focus on my life and purpose…..every now and again you have to refocus…. Thank you to those that have helped me to get my focus back by pouring into me what God told you to pour into me and you never knew why.

Self-Reflection
July 5, 2017

DOC's Corner

Disclaimer: Sorry this is not my usual inspirational message

"Why are you acting like that?"

I received a call on Saturday from an associate. I answered the phone politely with all the pleasantries. During our conversation, he asked what's wrong? Why are you being so submissive? What happened to your feistiness? After I stopped laughing at his use of submissive. I kindly asked what he was talking about. Apparently, I agreed with everything he was saying.

In fact, that question has been a common theme for me. Why are you acting like that? So, here's my answer.

At one point, I probably cared about you and now I just don't have the energy to deal with you or your drama. I'm at a point in my life where I know what I want and if you're not on board please step aside. If you feel threaten by YOUR perception of MY success, I'm sorry for you. I have never allowed my academic success to define me as a person. I have never thrown my academic success in anyone's face. I am who I am. I am feisty, sassy, sarcastic, blunt, loving, spoiled, …. I could go on but you get the picture. I am all

Nicole Harris

those things and more. I am 100% me at all times. I'm not acting any way. I am just reflecting what you give me!

Self-Reflection
August 2, 2017

Doc's Corner ~ Birthday Edition

Thank you to everyone that posted "Happy Birthday", called me, or texted me. Thank you to those that took me out for a special evening, for dinner, for the gorgeous flowers, and for the love. For those who left a meaningful message…. I'm glad I am in the land of the living to hear positive words. Each one of you made my day a little more special. I am truly thankful to see another day and turn another year younger!

What are you allowing into your life?

Let's take a look at social media… I once heard someone say that FB is depressing. What are you allowing on your timeline? Do you block certain contain? Do you block certain people? Let's take a stroll down my timeline…. I have the following:
- Happy Birthday wishes (positive)
- Saved & Single 5-day challenge (positive)
- Relaxer time (LOL)
- Staying thankful (positive)
- More Saved & Single 5-day challenge (positive – is this a hint)
- Michael Baisden (comedy)
- Praise the Lord (positive)
- Godly Dating (positive)
- Fibromyalgia (my life as a cover girl)

Readjusting My Crown

- Relationship Rules (positive)
- Black Therapist Rock!!! (positive)

Honestly, I thought I would have some crazy things on my timeline but I didn't. The list above is what I am allowing in my space…. From time to time I do see individuals asking to join their team and yes, I did at one time until I had a little talk with Jesus. Jesus told me that what God has for me is for me and He will open doors that no man can open or close. I want to leave this with you…. God created us to be happy and to enjoy life to the fullest while serving Him. Are you living life to the fullest? Are you happy? On this day, the start of a new year…. I am claiming my happiness, I'm letting go of negative people and things. I am claiming everything that has been stolen from me…God promised me double for my trouble. I will live life to the fullest…. Thank you again for stopping to say happy birthday.

~Dr. Nicole Harris♥♥♥♥~

Life
08/31/2017

Doc's Corner

Death all around me…..

As I sit listening to my colleagues grieve the death of a co-worker and share their stories about her…. I realized that people know when their days are numbered. After listening of course, I needed to let go of the baggage that was given to me…. I sat in silence for a while to process everything and reflect on death. My mind goes back to 2002 when I lost my dear sister… She was at the VA Hospital in Hampton and

I know for a fact that she knew her days were numbered. Darlene, my sister, asked to see all her family… we showed up but I showed out sitting on the hospital floor joking around only the way I know how… until she asked me to feed her some ice and she told her secret …. She was dying… as I feed her the ice I noticed her skin just falling off…. She quickly took my attention away from her being sick and she asked what perfume I was wearing… Bath & Body Works' Warm Vanilla Sugar… she said she loved the way it smelled. I only wear that scent when she is on my mind. Darlene knew it was time to let go but she didn't until our dad gave her permission to go. Fast forward to January 2017…. I wasn't there but if you knew my cousin you knew how it happened… My dear cousin Pam went home to glory…. She spoke to those who were unable to make it to TX to see her and she said her last "I love you" to them…. Her parents and brother went to TX to see her and they gave her permission to go.

As for today, I'm listening to the story about my colleague being in the hospital and asking to see certain people from the job. She was preparing those around her for her departure from this world……

Death is all around me… not only in the physical sense but we… I have experience death of a relationships, death of employment… Out of the deaths we experience, physical death of a love one hurts the most but I want you to understand that your love one is at peace…. No, we don't want them to go because we are selfish and we don't feel like it's their time. Honey, God don't make mistakes…their job was done…. God met them at the pearly gates and said well done (or so we hope).

Now death of a relationship… that can be difficult to deal with because we all want closure and you may not get closure in the way you want. You may not know why the relationship ended and it hurts. Please know that everyone is in your life for a reason whether it is a season or lifetime. Know when their time in your life is up and that they cannot go where you need to go. If you still need closure write a letter to them…..and rip it up. It's just for you.

Death of employment…. Smh… I'm still dealing with this one. But God and I had a conversation…. He continues to tell me you did what I needed you to do there and your time was up… I prepared you long before it happened but you did not listen… you wanted to do it your way. Your way was the hard way. I gained so much from that job and to be honest I was content but God…. God's plan for you is great than any plan you have for yourself

Death is all around me…. How will you handle it? I've decided to cry first and while I'm crying I'll praise God for His bridesmaids' Grace and Mercy. I'm not where I want to be but thank God I'm not where I use to be.

Self-Reflection
October 15, 2017 (not posted on FB)

I am NOT my hair

I am not my hair songbird India Arie released "I am not my hair" in 2006.

I am not trying to duplicate her at all….

In recent days, no in recent months I have realized that the last 2 years have been very difficult for me. I knew I use my hair as my outward expression of how I have been feeling. But what shocked me was that a man that I have only known for a short while called me out on cutting my hair. He asked me what was going on? Do I need an intervention? My initial thoughts were how do you have the right to come for me? …. Who told you? It was as if he was all in my life and I wanted him to have no parts of my life. Everyone thinks I have it all together but in reality, I am falling apart. I struggle with so much and no one knows. I struggle with self-esteem, I struggle with knowing my worth, I struggle with succeeding in this life…. I struggle with so much. Since everyone thinks I am so strong I have to conceal my pain… My only way to express my hurt, pain, discomfort is through my hair…. My outwardly expression. I have gone from shoulder length hair to a fade that in itself speaks volume. How do I get out of this rut? How do I heal? I will admit I am broken. I am not where I want to be… financially, career wise, or my love life and that bothers me every day. I feel broken every day. As for my love life…ha… I think I've being weighing my worth on how much he (yes Trey) loves me. This journey with him taught me that you first must love yourself before you can love anyone else. Ugh. I just want a man to love me unconditionally for me, to support me, to be my comforter, and the list goes on. Back to the question: how am I going to heal? Get back to the fundamentals.. get back to praising and worshipping God, to work on my interpersonal relationship with God, to love me, to go after my dreams, to continue therapy, to me the best me regardless of who is in my life.

Self-Reflection
12/24/2017

In a week, we will be preparing to end 2017 and anxiously bring in 2018. I honestly didn't think that I had it in me to reflect on 2017.... In my book, it is one of the most challenging years of my life. The beginning of 2017, I was trying to refocus on me and my foundation. I walked away from a job that I enjoyed but no longer productive. I believed that I cried for at least 2 months because I honestly did not know what to do. During this time, I submitted my resume and had interviews... all my job opportunities were contingent on me passing the NCMHCE (LPC) exam in February. Unfortunately, I did not pass and so those opportunities where no longer an option for me. Along with postponing my goal of becoming a LPC, my daughter had just informed me that she was expecting. In the mist of all of this, a potential employer saw my CV on indeed. I reluctantly, took the position but only for a short while until another opportunity came available. From this point, I believe I made a series of troubling decisions. In April, I went to Vegas with my beau. I had an awesome time with him. Only one thing bothered me and honestly still do.... After 4 years, my name is not saved in his phone. Well dang. I have yet to say anything. I thought about walking away but well.... Life goes on. I met some wonderful people and reconnected with some old friends. I participated in commencement and saw my students graduate with their bachelor degree. The summer was just awesome. Mixing old friends with new friends can be liberating. I used the summer to focus on me before becoming a Gigi (I'm way

Nicole Harris

too young to be a grandmother). I also used this time to be creative with my hair and chop it all off to go natural. My way of dealing with everything that was happening. I took the NCMHCE 2 more times and again missed them by 3 points and 14 points, respectively. My grandson was born in September. In October, I had the opportunity to speak about Mental Health and seniors... I felt so alive. I feel like I am in this tornado and I can't seem to get out. Yes, I had to some great moments in 2017 but I was unable to accomplish my dream... my goals in 2017. Life got absurd... I felt like nothing was going the way I wanted it to go. Yet, my faith said this too shall pass and God did not bring me this far to leave me. I realized that I no longer felt fulfilled by working for someone else. I am now trying to rediscover me and what makes me happy. Passing the NCMHCE will allow me to help others one-on-one, a way to open the door for more opportunities to speak about Mental Health.... Yes, 2017 was a rough one for me; so much happened so much death around me. I am looking forward to 2018, I pray that it will be great and that all my goals will be achieved.

Summary

We all need to do daily self-reflections, so we can learn from our mistakes. My transparent self-reflections have a common theme: God's grace and mercy. I'm still working on me and I will always work on me...refining myself is an ongoing process. I truly have had some good days and bad days... heck I have had two (2) extremely difficult years but all in all life has been good. These two years have made me more aware of who I am as an individual.

Self-Awareness

My self-awareness stems from being so enmeshed in the roles of mother and wife that I had to rediscover me, Nicole. Interesting enough I found, no I rediscovered me when I was working on my master's degree in community counseling. How ironic that I would rediscover who I was while learning my purpose in this world. It took me a while to be aware of myself and the baggage I carry around.

Self-Awareness
September 30, 2014

A friend and I was talking about "being ready" today. We all have said when I'm ready I'm going to do so and so or I will do that when I am ready. My friend simply said that sometimes being ready means having the right people beside you. Well, do you have the right people on your team? What are the criteria for being on your team? To be on my team (Team Nicole) you have to be one of my biggest fans, be honest, allow me to show my emotional nakedness.....just to name a few. #teamNicole

Mental Illness
May 11, 2016

Doc's Corner

Someone said something that bothered my spirit as it relates to depression and suicide. I'm not sure if they knew that I was in the mental health field but nevertheless the comment was insensitive. Everyone deals with situations differently... some need to process things a little longer, some need to seek therapy (it's okay), some are okay the next day.... To say get over it is insensitive. We all have dealt with something in our lives that we can't just get over "it". Depression is real! Mental Illness is real! Our babies are killing themselves.... suicide is the 10th leading cause of death in America for all ages. So no, they cannot "just get over it." Please stop judging people and their situation instead take the time to get to understand their perception because their perception is their reality!!! #counselingworks#mentalillnessisnolaughingmatter

Self-Awareness
January 29, 2017

Doc's Corner

Self-awareness
As January 2017 comes to an end, I am still refocusing. I acknowledge that I am not perfect; that I have a ton of flaws; that sometimes I become too involved too passion about things; and that I keep things to myself until I explode. Daily, we should be on a journey to self-awareness.

I want to share a few things with you.

1. Keep your faith. Always remember that our Heavenly Father cannot lie and He has promised us so much. Sometimes in life you must step out on FAITH and allow God to take the wheel!! (which means you MUST let go of the wheel)

2. God's plan is so much greater than any plan you have dreamed of for yourself. Ask for guidance from HIM and HE will guide your path.

3. Understand your purpose…. Have a little talk with Jesus

4. Always always be genuinely YOU. God created you UNIQUELY to be you. Don't let anyone change you…… however, please know that it is a time, a place for everything know how to turn "it" on and off as needed. No façade.

5. Do what you love, what you are passionate about it should connect to #'s 2 & 3.

6. Know your worth!! Don't downgrade or settle because someone isn't ready to pay you your worth…… On the same token know when your time is up at a particular place…. Some things have an expiration date

7. You can't share your dreams and goals with everyone. Just because you are not a crab in a barrel doesn't being others aren't.

8. Be humble. No matter what happens to you good, bad, or indifferent someone will talk about you.

9. TRUE friends will be there during the rough/hard times.

10. Every day tell God all about your troubles, thank HIM, tell HIM your wants/needs … Just make it plain.

Just Doc's thoughts…… think about it

Nicole Harris

Self-Awareness
March 8, 2017

Doc's Corner:

No matter what we do the question is always "why". Can you answer your why's?

Why do you keep going to school?

~I have two beautiful daughters that I want to instill that knowledge is power.~

Why do you have a doctorate degree?

~ God created me to do greater than I could ever dream of and my destiny requires me to have it.~

Why are you so emotional?

~My emotions prove that I am human and shows my daughters, nieces, nephews, and god children that even the strong have emotions .....it's a sign of great strength.~

Why are you angry?

~I'm not. I'm just a matter of fact person who does not know how to sugar coat things. I see your potential and push you to your destiny.~

What are your why's and your response?

Self-Awareness
August 23, 2017

Doc's Corner

Who's taking care of me?

Last week, I was told that I am always giving & taking care of others. True. Then I was asked the hardest question: "Who takes care of you?"

I really had to think about it. No one takes care of me. This lead to the next question: "Why?" My answer: everyone assumes that I am strong and I can handle what life throws at me. But the truth is that I wish someone would take the time to ask how I'm doing, to be concerned about my well-being, to take care of me, to give me a hug, to love on me.....and most importantly stop assuming I can handle everything. I guess I have to wait on my prince charming.

~~~the one's that give the most are the ones that need it the most~~~

Self-Awareness
August 31, 2017

While Doc's Corner stems from my personal issues...it is rare that I directly say them.... this last week as been trying for me... to see my high school sweetheart in the hospital and my children deeply impacted by his illness.... has brought out...confirmed part of my purpose in this world. My role is to take care of, intercede, stand in the gaps,......to be a blessing by advocating for those who cannot. He and I made a vow on 5/26/2001 until death due us part....in this world we ended our union in 2012 but those vows are still written in heaven.

You never know what you are capable of doing until you have no other choice. You are even stronger and wiser when you have a choice and choose to do what is RIGHT. But God...

Nicole Harris

Summary

As I work on this accumulation of my ideas, I am currently struggling with my purpose and my why. It's clear that I know my purpose and my why but what troubles me is the journey to get to my destiny. This journey to my ultimate purpose is the hardest thing I had to do. I feel as if I have been beaten up in all facets of life. I know God's plan is greater than mine and He never fails. If it wasn't for God, I would not have achieved everything that I have achieved.

Achievement

At this point in my life, one would think that I have achieved all my goals. Well, I aim high. Yes, I have a terminal degree … Doctorate of Education but I haven't reached all my goals. Earlier on in life I wanted to be an attorney and later it would be a probation officer. After a 3-year tenure working in a local jail, I quickly changed my mind. I decided to go into the mental health field. Never in a million years did I ever imagine that I, Nicole Harris, would become Dr. Harris. While I worked extremely hard to become Dr. Harris… I haven't begun to walk in my purpose, not yet. This is a little insight into this journey as Dr. Harris as I prepare to walk in my purpose. I just need to readjust my crown and put on my matching stilettos. God is preparing me for something great. Through this journey, I pray that I can stay humble.

Achievement
January 8, 2016

Doc's Corner......

Achiever versus Title Chasers
One of my job responsibilities is to promote, demote,

or terminate individuals. I want to focus on the promoted individuals and their pride. I noticed there at two types of people the achiever and the title chaser. Let's talk about the two.

The title chaser allows their title to go to their head for example the administrative assistant that is promoted to the office administrator. Hmmm.... Sounds like the same skill set with more responsibilities. The title chaser will think and behave as if they have more authority since they are the office administrator. They may think they can make administrative decisions. They also feel the need to question the administrators of the agency. They feel like they should be in the middle of every conversation and know ever decision that is made in the agency. The title chasers feel like they are better than everyone else to the point that they put other people down. They are chasing a title.... you see the title makes them feel important. The title could be lead case worker, case manager, program director, etc. no matter the title they feel important because they have this particular title.

Then there are the achievers. I like to have achievers on my team. They don't let the title go to their head. The achievers are only concerned with what their job duties and responsibilities are as well as the tools they need to get the job done. They never flaunt or boast their title. Nine times out of ten, they are team players. Achievers want to know what they can do to help the agency and the team to achieve the organizational goals. They are interested in professional growth and the growth of the agency.

Let's make this a little personal....and change the milieu. I believe that a title chaser takes that mentality into their home. You know the type, I bring home the bacon, I run this house…. yes that person…they are a title chaser. Now the achiever, will be like this is our money…my title is how I make the money.

Let's add gender…. A woman that is a title chaser will tell her boyfriend, fiancé, or husband that the money she brings home is all hers and will ask him, what does he have to bring to the table with his broke self. A woman that is an achiever, will say honey what do we need to do. The achiever will never throw her achievements in her significant others life. The woman achiever will be the submissive woman at home and would think nothing of her degrees or accolades at home.

I know you are waiting for the personal part…..well here it goes…At work I am Dr. Nicole Harris. I just happen to be the program director…..which means I work my butt off and nothing more. At home, I'm Nicole, mom, and some call me Nikkie…..my accomplishments have nothing to do with my personal life. Let me change that my professional accomplishments are the ways I show my daughters that anything is possible….I am their tangible role model. But at home I am not Dr. Nicole Harris….I am just Nicole, a woman that have achieved many things.

~Dr. Nicole Harris ~

Achievements
January 10, 2016

It was worth it!!!

I get asked a lot, was it (receiving my doctorate) worth it? Absolutely, it was worth it. I became a tangible role model for my daughters, nieces, nephews, and godchildren. I will be able to show the world that a teenage mother can overcome the stigma. This woman has overcome numerous obstacles and it wasn't easy but it was worth it. Today, edifies why it was worth it. My nephew came over and saw my doctorate degree. He just stared at it in complete awe. I asked him what was wrong. He said he couldn't believe that his aunt was a doctor. Of course, I am laughing because I know to him I will always be his crazy aunt NeNe. To see that his aunt NeNe is a doctor amazes him. So if you ask me was obtaining my doctorate worth the time, sacrifice, tears, dedication and struggle…. I will tell you without a doubt without hesitation….YES, it was worth it. I pray that I am able to encourage my nephews, niece, godchildren, and my daughters to aim high!!! #itsworthitall

Achievement
May 9, 2016

Doc's Corner:

I'm trying to stay off my soapbox but sometimes people need to hear the truth. I'm debating between "A closed mouth don't get feed" and "Ask and you shall receive".

The worse answer anyone can give you is "NO"….it's up to you to decide what to do with that "no".

Achievement
November 13, 2016

Doc's Corner:

At some point in our lives we all feel as if we have fallen short of our goal. I believe that this happens because we try to fit into a box that the world/society say we should be in. If you have "x" title you should behave and be this way and if you have "y" title you should behave and act another way. Well, I was not created to fit neatly in a box. I was created to stand out and be uniquely me….an unorthodox woman of God. My purpose is to bring people to God by being

uniquely me….if I was any other way I would not be able to capture the attention of the people God create me to capture. Remember God created you for a purpose use your talent and who you are to manifest your purpose.

Achievements
March 7, 2017

Doc's Corner:

Let me be transparent for a minute. I love what I do and I honestly have no problem sharing anything that I have. I don't like to be in the lime light…. I'm the "background singer"

My love language is words of affirmation. Recently, a few people have told me thank you for all that I have done for them, taught them, and modeled for them. I am overwhelmed with emotions. Especially when all I heard from others is that I am mean and angry all the time. No, I just want you to do your job and be the best you can be…..

For those who have called me and gave me words of affirmation….. Thank you. I will end this post with the words for the person I least thought would say a kind word to me

"You are a teacher to those who teach." #humbled #blessed #thankful

Nicole Harris

Achievements
November 14, 2017

I have been processing what I want to do with my life. I realized that (1) I do not want to work for anyone else and (2) I want to use my skill set to train and teach others. I want to teach in higher education as well as going around the world to educate the mass on mental illness hence me needing my LPC. I also want to continue to conduct outpatient therapy sessions. I feel more productive on Friday than any other day of the week. I also believe in the holistic approach; therefore, I need to focus back on my spirituality. I believe that I was created to intertwine the secular world and spirituality.

Summary

I am forever thankful for all my achievements and my supporters. My achievements are truly mine, I sometimes sit at awe that I have achieved the unthinkable. I become sadden when I am unable to accomplish the one thing that I want more than anything else. I am proud that I am Dr. Harris but I want three (3) more letters behind my name. I am not sure of God's plan, but it has to be great. I know it's mine but this struggle to obtain my LPC has to have a purpose. I've came so close yet so far. Again, I am super proud of my accomplishments. Someone told me to look at my resume, so I did. I have had positions that proves that I have the knowledge and know how to do the job. I will get my LPC in due time… I'm just readjusting my crown.

Conclusion

I pray that this book gives you inspiration to keep moving, keep dreaming, to motivate yourself, and to live your life by your own definition. No one said life would be easy but I promise it is all worth it. This book covers several years from 2008 to the present (2018). I have grown in these 10 years, I am no longer that little insecure woman that I use to be but I am Dr. Nicole Harris. You see in 10 years I went from enmeshed in my roles as a mother and wife to this phenomenal woman that dares to be different. I have made decisions that only make sense to me; well the truth be told some don't even make sense to me. What I know is when God says move please move and be obedient. My life is far from what I want it to be but a lot better than it use to be. I am a daughter, sister, aunt, mother, gigi, friend, and the list goes on. Most importantly, I became a tangible hero for my daughters. My faith keeps me grounded even when I wanted to run away or when I feel depleted and defeated.

About the Author

Nicole Harris

Dr. Nicole Harris is a clinical supervisor for a community based mental health program. She is also an associate professor at local university. Dr. Harris has a diverse background in the human service field from a deputy sheriff to program director.

For almost 17 years, Dr. Harris has utilized her talent and passion by helping others with their behavioral and emotional issues. Dr. Harris has developed an effective background in the clinical realm with a professional style that promotes and empowers her counseling staff to increase their professional growth while accomplishing their personal goals. Dr. Harris is able to meet her clientele at their emotional, spiritual, and behavioral levels which enables her to better assist the clients with their individual needs by focusing on each individual need.

Dr. Harris received her Doctorate in Education from Argosy University in 2015. Her dissertation focused on successful community reintegration. Dr. Harris went back to school in 2008 to work towards another degree, to ensure that she was eligible for supervision as a resident in counseling to become a Licensed Professional Counselor. In 2010, Dr. Harris received an Educational Specialist degree from Hampton University in Community Counseling. In 2008, she received a Master of Arts from Norfolk State University in Urban Education – Community Counseling. Dr. Harris has earned certificates as a Certified Substance Abuse Counselor, Certified Rehabilitation Provider and Human Service Board Certified Practitioner. Dr. Harris has a Bachelor of Arts from Norfolk State University in Sociology with emphasize on Criminal Justice.

Dr. Harris is passionate about empowering women, advocating for the mentally ill, educating her community about mental illness, and assisting felons with getting their rights restored as well as implementing an effective program to assist the previously incarcerated with successful reintegration.

When Dr. Harris is not working, she enjoys spending time with her sister, sister-in-law, friends, daughters, and grandson. She enjoys spending time at the park or the beach.

Nicole Harris

Printed in the United States
By Bookmasters